The Puppy Who Refused To Die

Paul Lockinger

$\mathcal{FV}$
$\mathcal{F}$lorian $\mathcal{V}$alentine Publishing
Mesa, AZ
www.florianvalentine.com

The Puppy Who Refused To Die.

Published by *F*lorian *V*alentine Publishing
3032 S. Paseo Loma Circle
Mesa, AZ. 85202

Visit our website at www.florianvalentine.com

First Printing 2008
Printed in the United States of America
By Signature Book Printing, www.sbpbooks.com

ISBN 978-0-615-21621-8

Quantity discounts are available on bulk
purchases of this book for educational, gift,
fund raising, or other publisher approved
purposes. Special books or book excerpts may be
created to fit specific needs.

For more information please contact the publisher
at info@florianvalentine.com.

About the Cover

The cover picture was taken near the end of February in 2008. It is a picture of Green (The puppy who refused to die) five months before his third birthday.

Green was told that we needed a good picture of him for the front cover of his book. Green sat up, allowed one picture, and then ran off to play.

Fortunately, it was a good picture.

Becker College

Acknowledgments

It was through the actions of the wonderful and caring volunteer members of the rescue organization that I came to live with my new mom and dad, Sue and Paul.

When I was sick, the volunteers would be there to care for me through prayers, donations, or again giving their time. They would be there for Mom and Dad too, as they needed support as much as I did.

The volunteers would be there when I was well with treats, and toys, or just to visit for awhile. They came bearing gifts for me, my sisters and brothers, Comet, Bro, Bumpkin, and Tiger the cat. Often, they would have something for Mom and Dad too.

There have been so many volunteers that have touched my life, many who I have never met, and many who have been there by my side. The rescue volunteers who I remember most are Karen, Daniel, Andrea, Amber, Fred, Joyce, Kas, Tammy, Linda, Laura, Jeff, LJ, Jenny, Joey, Kyle, Tim, and Michele.

I do not wish to thank just these individuals. I want to thank everyone who has played a part in my life. Thank you, one and all.

Contents

Introduction............................... ix

Puppy Pictures............................. xii

Chapter 1 A Bad Start...................... 1

Chapter 2 Our New Homes.................... 4

Chapter 3 I Meet Doctor Anna.............. 10

Chapter 4 Puppies Everywhere............. 17

Chapter 5 Mom and Dad Get A Break........ 23

Chapter 6 Hope Returns................... 31

Chapter 7 Snap, Crackle, And Pop........ 39

Chapter 8 I See A Specialist............ 42

Chapter 9 Where Have All The Puppies Gone..... 47

Chapter 10 Not Quite My Birthday......... 53

Chapter 11 The New Medicine.............. 56

Chapter 12 Who Am I...................... 58

Chapter 13 Green Grows Up................ 69

Chapter 14 Is This The End.............. 75

Animal Rescue............................ 83

Appendix I Charts........................ 86

Appendix II E-Mails...................... 96

Appendix III Definitions.................... 106

From the Author........................... 109

Book Order Blank.......................... 113

Pictures

Brown, White, Grey, and Green................. 5
Dark Purple, Red, Cream, Lavender, and Blue.... 5
Sleeping with my sister and brothers.......... 13
Brown wanted to know if he measures up........ 13
Sue and Andrea feeding a puppy................ 14
Amber holding a puppy......................... 14
Red gets comfortable.......................... 15
Bro is in charge.............................. 15
Bedtime with the alligator.................... 16
Snoopy makes a good pillow.................... 16
Faith and her puppies......................... 21
Faith's three puppies......................... 21
Hope and her puppies.......................... 22
Hope's seven puppies.......................... 22
Who left this plate of milk here.............. 25
Comet and Bro learn to supervise.............. 25
This divider is just the right height......... 26
I think I will cover up for awhile............ 26
Rub a dub dub, Time for a scrub............... 27
I prefer a brush, but Dad likes the comb...... 27
Seems like all we do is sleep................. 28
When we are not eating of course.............. 28
We need a basket to go to the doctor's now.... 29
Attacking Comet might be a good idea.......... 29
Two plates of food might be enough............ 30
Hey, it's my turn to lay in the bowl of food.. 30
Puppy pile on the stuffed toys................ 33
Give me that rope bone........................ 33
I can sleep on Amber's shoulder............... 34
Andrea's got me, what can I do................ 34
Free to sleep in the dining room.............. 35
It's pretty comfortable on this back porch.... 35
I love my stuffed animals..................... 36

Relaxing with the stuffed toys................ 36
This belly makes a nice soft headrest......... 37
Look out, sponge bob is attacking............. 37
One stick for three puppies................... 38
Togetherness is good.......................... 38
I am getting a treatment...................... 40
Look out, In coming........................... 45
Is there room for one more.................... 45
The fresh air just knocks us out.............. 46
Let's line up in the bedroom.................. 46
Grey, now called Honey........................ 49
Red, Became known as Gus...................... 49
Sammy, I knew him as Cream.................... 50
Yellow, Decided her name should be Maggie..... 50
Maroon, Wanted to be known as Charm........... 51
Orchid, Went with a Christmas name (Holly).... 51
Pink, Changed her name to Zoe................. 52
Orange, We now call Orange Bumpkin or Bump.... 52
My eyes have not opened yet................... 61
This is a nice soft blanket................... 61
I have my own saucer of milk.................. 62
What a comfortable spot....................... 62
What are you holding me up for................ 63
I am climbing out of the tunnel............... 63
What.. 64
Me and my alligator pillow.................... 64
This bed is a good place for a puppy.......... 65
Breathe in, Breathe out....................... 65
I am the king of the table.................... 66
Water is good, baths are bad.................. 66
What are you looking at....................... 67
You can call me mud dog....................... 67
What's a puppy got to do to get a belly rub... 68
Bump is always getting in my face............. 68
What's up Mom................................. 71
I can twist like a snake...................... 71
I'm going to school with the kids............. 72
King of the couch............................. 72
Relaxing on the back patio.................... 73
It's my stuffed duck.......................... 73
I'll just stay in the bathroom................ 74
I really don't feel good...................... 74
Paul with Green............................... 109

Introduction

The following email was sent by Sue. It is through the quick actions of Sue and the other volunteers that I have a story to tell.

Many emails were sent, only a few are included in this book. The emails have been edited into a form that is usable in this printing, but all pertinent information remains intact.

Many names and email addresses have been left out to protect the privacy of those involved. You will see a couple of e-mails within the story itself; others that document details have been included in Appendix II at the back of the book.

Introduction

From: Sue
Sent: Friday, July 22, 2005 2:58 p.m.

Subject: Heads up for a HUGE intake

I just got a call from Bonny. The Pima County Animal Control (PCAC) just shut down a puppy mill in Tucson. Bonny went to do her normal shelter walk and discovered Golden after Golden after Golden at (PCAC).

One mom with twelve pups and still might deliver one more — number thirteen was stillborn — all look pure.

One mom with ten pups two days old — a couple of the pups look like lab mix.

Four or five other pregnant females — the Pima County Animal Control (PCAC) veterinarian is evaluating to see if she/he will abort any of these litters depending on how far along the pregnancies are and what condition the expectant moms are in.

There are seven other possible Goldens to come in.

The (PCAC) veterinarian is still trying to evaluate the dogs to see what condition they are all in. She/he is also trying to determine what kind of charges are going to be filed so they
x

know if they can release any of the
dogs. The charges filed will probably be
felony charges, as many of the other
dogs show signs of abuse.

There were many other dogs of different
breeds besides the Goldens.

I'm not sure who should be in charge of
this. Sarah as Southern AZ Director or
Joyce as Second Vice President is my
guess. Peg and Kathy I'm including you
in this note as you are on rotation this
week for your teams. Kathy don't panic I
will help once we find out what is going
on for sure. I'm sure Mary would take a
mom and her pups.

Bonny said I was the first one that
answered the phone. I am including Bonny
in this note too as I told her I would
so she can correct any errors I made.
She said we would definitely be getting
the two moms with pups but she didn't
know when yet.

Puppy Pictures

This is my story; the true story of Green, the puppy who refused to die. I wrote it myself with a little help from my Dad, Paul Lockinger.

Although many puppy pictures were taken while we were with our foster mom and dad, Sue and Paul, I have only included those that I felt gave the best pictorial history of the development of my brothers, my sister, and myself.

I have also included a few pictures of Faith, Hope, and their puppies. There may be one or two of my big brothers, Comet and Bro in here too.

The pictures scattered throughout the book were taken by my Mom and Dad (Sue and Paul).

Let's get started reading. I will show you the way.

THE

PUPPY

WHO

REFUSED

TO

DIE

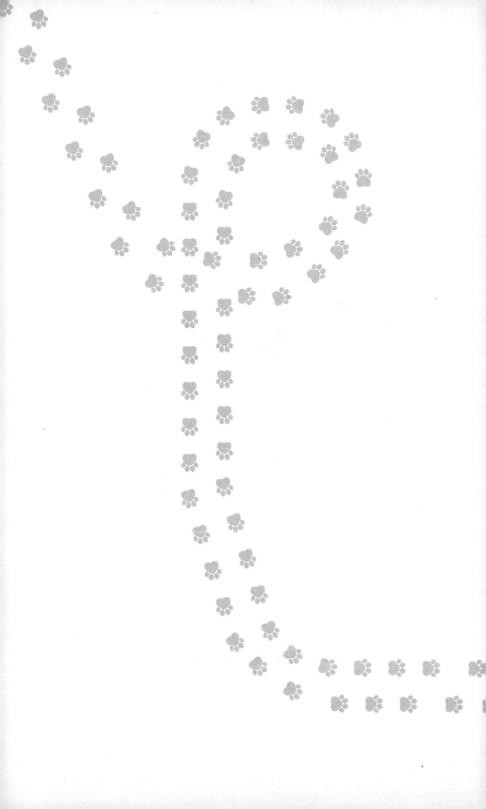

1

A Bad Start

I was born near Tucson, Arizona in July of 2005 to a very young mother who rejected her entire litter. My first days of life were spent at the Pima County Animal Control facility where I fought to survive along side of my brothers, sisters, and another litter of puppies whose mother had also rejected them. Many of my brothers and sisters, along with members of the other litter, passed away during our stay at the animal control facility. It was through no fault of the workers that many of us would not survive.

We were born as a result of breeding at a puppy mill in the Tucson area. Some of you may have heard about puppy mills, for those of you that have not, let me tell you what I know about them.

A puppy mill is a bad place for a dog. They exist only for the purpose of mass breeding and creating a source of income for their owners. The puppy mill owners have little or no interest in the lives or welfare of their dogs.

A Bad Start

The dogs that live at these places spend their entire lives in a cage with no human companionship. They never get to lie on a bed; there are no toys or treats. Medical care is often ignored.

The dogs are bred continuously for years, and when their fertility wanes, they are abandoned, or put to death.

The poor conditions at the puppy mill, and the lack of care provided to my mother, as well as that of the other mother, had resulted in two litters of puppies in poor health. So many puppies needing more care than the workers at the Pima County Animal Control facility could handle.

It was Sunday, July 31, eleven days since the first of us had been born. Our numbers had quickly dwindled from twenty-two to only nine.

Any glimmer of hope was fading when suddenly, I saw her appear out of nowhere. She was carrying a small basket filled with soft fabric leaving just enough room for nine little puppies.

Bonny, a volunteer for a Golden Retriever rescue organization came in and scooped up all nine of us.

Bonny, along with Sarah, took our now united litter on a ride to Casa Grande, AZ where we met with Joyce and Mike; all were volunteer members of the same rescue organization.

One of the rescuers found formula and little bottles to use on the way to our new homes. At the Wendy's parking lot in Casa Grande we had our first meal as the newest and smallest members of this rescue organization.

During our brief stay at the Wendy's parking lot, I overheard the volunteers talking about us. One volunteer said that a normal Golden Retriever puppy should weigh fourteen to eighteen ounces at birth. Another volunteer said that she would have expected each of us to be two or more pounds by now.

All the volunteers agreed that at almost two weeks of age, none of us were near the weight that we should be.

After our meal we continued on our trip to Mesa, AZ, now riding with Joyce and Mike. The next stop on our trip was to be at the home of Sue and Paul.

2

Our New Homes

At Sue and Paul's there was a warm bed with clean blankets and heat lamps. Two extra large Golden Retrievers, named Comet and Bro, greeted us with licks and nudges. More members of the rescue group were there to prepare us for our stay. We were cleaned with warm water baths and marked with colored ribbon around our necks.

Before we were allowed to eat again we were all weighed and charts were started to keep track of our progress; the charts are included in Appendix I in the back of this book. I was marked with a Green ribbon and my weight was said to be fourteen and one-half ounces. At my five p.m. feeding I gobbled up fifteen milliliters (ML) of formula. Just in case you do not know, that is one whole tablespoon.

The colors marking my brothers were Red, who was twelve and one-half ounces; Dark Purple, Cream and Brown, who weighed thirteen ounces each. My sisters were marked as Blue, who was the smallest at only 10 ounces, Lavender and

The Puppy Who Refused To Die

White weighing ten and one-half ounces each, and Grey who was as big as some of the boys at a whopping 13 ounces.

   As you can see, I was the biggest one of the bunch.

Brown, White, Grey and I all stayed with Sue and Paul, our new Mom and Dad.

Dark Purple, Red, Cream, Lavender, and Blue all went home with Mary, another foster parent for the rescue group.

Our New Homes

    Just four days later, on August 04, 2005 Red and Cream came back to live with us bringing with them some very sad news. Dark Purple, Lavender, and Blue had all passed away. Our numbers now were lowered to only six.

    Red, at fourteen and one-half ounces, and Cream at fourteen ounces were the only puppies showing improvement during these first few days. Besides the loss of three from the litter, the weight of the remaining puppies was less than or the same as it had been when the volunteers rescued us. Brown and I remained at our original weights of thirteen and fourteen and one-half ounces respectively. Grey had lost one-half of an ounce and White was now down to only nine and one-half ounces.

    On each of the next two days I would hear that unmistakable whine that preceded the death of so many of my litter mates. On August 05, just before eight a.m., my sister, White, let out her final whimper. Then, early in the morning on August 06, Brown left us. We were now only four, one girl and three boys.

    Until now very few members of the rescue group knew of our existence. On Sunday, August 07, an email was sent by the president of the group informing the entire membership of the rescue of many and the survival of only four.

**Here is what
the membership was told.**

Some volunteers have been keeping a situation quiet for a week now. They felt the need to do this until they could assess and determine exactly what they were dealing with and what they could expect.

Now they feel they should share this information and ask everyone to combine all the positive energy that they have seen work so well when many rescue volunteers join together.

Many of us were high on life, as the Harvest of Gold puppy mills dogs were brought into rescue, and joined their forever families. A puppy mill had closed and Goldens were welcomed into loving arms.

Recently there was another puppy-mill closure; this time in our own state. Dogs of all breeds were confiscated and taken into state custody. There is a criminal investigation currently being conducted.

Two very young Golden mothers were among this group. Together they whelped twenty two puppies.

Circumstances beyond anyone's control forced the puppies to remain in state custody until last Sunday. By then there were only nine. They were only a week old. The mothers of these two litters could not be released due to the continuing investigation.

Volunteers retrieved these puppies in a heartbeat. They were small and extremely weak. These puppies were put into the care of two of the very best foster families, who gave up their sleep, daily tasks, and put their own lives on hold to nurture these tiny babies. This was a HUGE undertaking

The two families fed puppies every two to three hours, twenty four/seven. The families monitored each puppy's food intake, temperature, weights and also stimulated them to make sure they eliminated.

They held perfectly formed beautiful pups for the last time as they said goodbye. It meant drying the tears for the ones that were gone and focusing to save the ones that were still with us.

There are four puppies still with us; their names are Green, Red, Grey, and Cream. At the present time, the puppies seem to be holding their own.

Under the guidance of the veterinarians, it is understood that the two families are doing all that can be done for the puppies.

Whether or not they will survive is not within our control. We ask that you please keep them in your prayers along with the people who are trying so hard to save them.

The Puppy Who Refused To Die

The message ended by stating that
updates will be sent every few days.

3

I Meet Doctor Anna

My first visit to the doctor was on August 01, 2005 in the afternoon. It was a short trip from our new home in Mesa to the animal clinic in Chandler, AZ. White, Grey, Brown and I were loaded into a cat carrier that seemed way too big for the four of us and off we went with Mom and Dad.

At the doctor's office there were lots of new people and an old friend. I remember meeting Joyce the day before when she brought us from Casa Grande to our new home with Sue and Paul. She helped give us baths and fed us, both on our trip and at our new home.

I learned that Joyce was the Second Vice President and the Veterinarian Coordinator for the rescue organization. Because of the positions she held with the group, it was up to her to make all the decisions about our health care. Joyce was to learn a lot about us today and make some very important decisions.

The Puppy Who Refused To Die

We were all locked up in a little room - Mom, Dad, Joyce, White, Grey, Brown, and ME. People kept coming in and out of the room using a different door than they had led us through. All of these people would come into the room and poke or prod at us, write something in a folder, and leave through that other door. Mom and Dad said these were the vet techs. After some time the vet techs were done with us and one said, "The doctor will be in to see you soon", as she left through that other door.

After what seemed like a very long wait, the doctor came into the room. She used that other door just like all the vet techs and introduced herself as Dr. Anna. She talked with Mom, Dad and Joyce for a few minutes and then went right to work poking, prodding and writing in the folder just like the vet techs. When Dr. Anna was done examining my brother, sisters and me, we were put back into the cat carrier and headed for home.

On the way home, Mom and Dad made a stop at the pharmacy to pick up medicine for all of us puppies. Mom and Dad were told that we needed an over-the-counter medicine to treat us for coccidiosis. We were all given some of the medicine that evening and then we had to wait a few days before we could have any more.

I Meet Doctor Anna

     I had no idea what this coccidiosis
thing was. My friend Joyce said she
would check it out on the internet, and
let me know what she found out.
     It was not long before Joyce sent
me an E-mail with all the information
she had located about coccidiosis. I
have included the information in
Appendix III located at the back of this
book.
     I think this is a good spot for
some pictures.

The Puppy Who Refused To Die

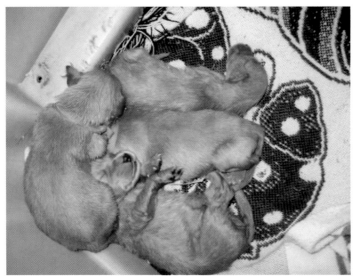

August 01, 2005
Sleeping with my sister and brothers

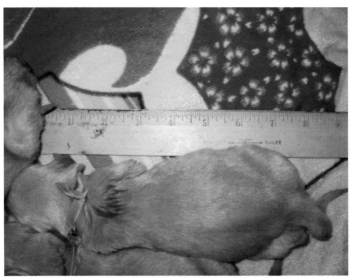

August 04, 2005
Brown wanted to know if he measures up

I Meet Doctor Anna

August 04, 2005
Sue and Andrea feeding a puppy

August 04, 2005
Amber holding a puppy

The Puppy Who Refused To Die

August 05, 2005
Red gets comfortable

August 06, 2005
Bro is in charge

August 07, 2005
Bedtime with the alligator

August 07, 2005
Snoopy makes a good pillow

4

Puppies Everywhere

For awhile all was good. We ate and
we slept. We ate and we grew. We ate and
we played. The eating was the most
important part of our day.

One night, Mom and Dad started to
bring in dog crates and exercise pens.
As they filled them with blankets, I
knew something was up. Our spot was in
the dining room near the back door. The
new crates and exercise pens were set up
on the other side of the room with a
table and chairs in between.

It was in the evening, on August
18, 2005, that it happened. I know
because it was dark outside. The carport
door opened and in walked a momma dog
named Faith. Her three puppies were
close behind. Then, in walked another
momma dog named Hope. Hope brought seven
puppies with her.

As I watched, all the people who
had come with these two momma dogs and
their puppies burst into action. All the
new puppies were cleaned, weighed, and
marked with colored yarn. The momma dogs

Puppies Everywhere

and their puppies were carefully and
lovingly settled into their crates.
    The following chart lists the
weights of the puppies as recorded on
the evening of August 18, 2005. The
weights of Faith and Hope are from a
veterinarian visit on August 19, 2005.

Name	Sex	Weight
Faith	Female Momma Dog	35#
Black	Male	1# 14 oz
Navy	Male	1# 14 oz
Hunter	Male	2# 2 oz
Hope	Female Momma Dog	33.5#
Maroon	Female	1# 1 oz
Yellow	Female	15 oz
Pink	Female	13.5 oz
Mint	Female	12 oz
Orange	Male	1# 1 oz
Orchid	Female	13 oz
Smoke	Male	11 oz

    Comet and Bro, the huge Goldens
that had greeted us when we arrived,
tried to greet the new mommas and their
puppies. The puppies seemed to be okay
with the idea, but Faith and Hope did
not want Comet and Bro near their
territory. Faith and Hope did not even
like each other invading their space.
There was a lot of snarling going on and

The Puppy Who Refused To Die

I was staying as far away from it as I could get.

It was clear to me from the start that those two momma dogs did not like being where they were, but it took Mom and Dad a little longer to catch on. It was not long before all the new puppies and their mommas disappeared to other rooms in the house.

It took only a few days to find new homes for Faith, Hope, and all the new puppies. They moved on, but it would not be long before we would see some of them again.

Here are some pictures of Faith, Hope, and their puppies.

Puppies Everywhere

The Puppy Who Refused To Die

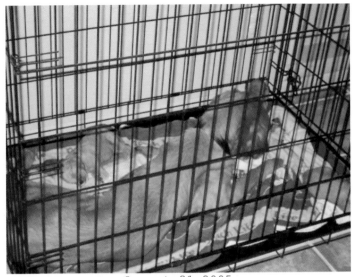

August 21,2005
Faith and her puppies

August 21,2005
Faith's three puppies

Puppies Everywhere

August 21,2005
Hope and her puppies

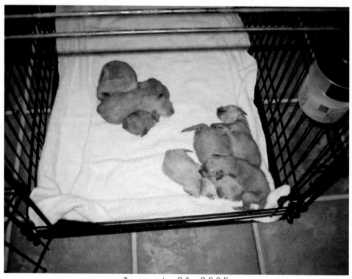

August 21,2005
Hope's seven puppies

5

Mom And Dad Get A Break

We were about four weeks old and Mom and Dad had been caring for us night and day since our arrival. Mom and Dad needed to go away on business. They had to go to another state. Mom said she was going for rest and relaxation. Dad said they were going to Illinois.

Before Mom and Dad left, Karen and Daniel visited, bringing with them two little girls named Andrea and Amber. Karen, Daniel, Andrea and Amber came over to learn how to care for us while Mom and Dad were gone.

They learned how to feed us from the bottles and how to feed us with saucers of milk, canned food, and kibble. They learned how to clean us up after we made the usual mess with our food. Most importantly, they learned how much we needed to spend time out of our enclosure. We needed to spend time with the big dogs Comet and Bro, and time to play with the people around us.

Mom And Dad Get A Break

Karen, Daniel, Andrea, and Amber came back to stay with us while Mom and Dad were away. We hardly noticed Mom and Dad were gone and we knew they would be back. The two little girls were fun to play with, and it was easy to steal some of their food. These little girls played near us on the floor and set down whatever they were eating. When they turned around, it was gone.

It was not a very long time until Mom and Dad came back home. Karen, Daniel, Andrea, and Amber learned the joys of caring for and playing with young puppies. They also learned it was hard work to care for just a few puppies, even for a short time.

Now, Karen and Daniel were ready for a break. Mom and Dad had been to Illinois, and Mom said she got some rest and relaxation while she was there. Now it was time for life to return to normal.

I think it is a good time for some more pictures.

The Puppy Who Refused To Die

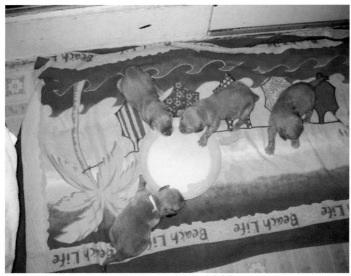

August 11, 2005
Who left this plate of milk here

August 12, 2005
Comet and Bro learn to supervise

Mom And Dad Get A Break

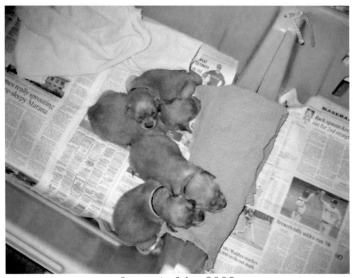

August 14, 2005
This divider is just the right height

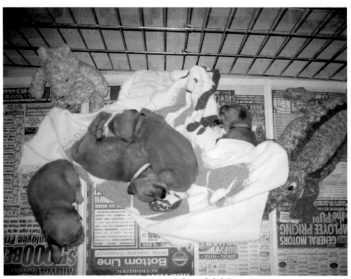

August 18, 2005
I think I will cover up for awhile

The Puppy Who Refused To Die

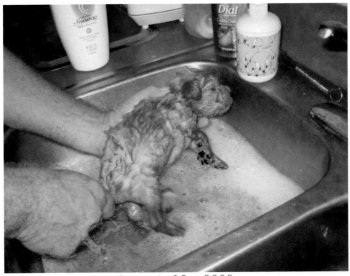

August 18, 2005
Rub a Dub Dub, time for a scrub

August 18, 2005
I prefer a brush, but Dad likes the comb

Mom And Dad Get A Break

August 20, 2005
Seems like all we do is sleep

August 23, 2005
When we are not eating of course

The Puppy Who Refused To Die

August 25, 2005
We need a basket to go to the Doctor's now

August 27, 2005
Attacking Comet might be a good idea

Mom And Dad Get A Break

August 30, 2005
Two plates of food might be enough

August 30, 2005
Hey, it's my turn to lay in the bowl of food

6

Hope Returns

It was near the end of September when Hope and her puppies came back to live with us. She was still very protective of her litter and did not want us near her or her puppies.

By now we were pretty active and had since graduated to using the doggie door just like Comet and Bro. Mom and Dad had placed bricks at the outside to help us reach the door easily.

At first, Hope and her puppies were kept in the office and were only allowed outside when we were locked in. Over time we were all allowed to be together and we got along without fighting.

Sadly, Hope lost some of her litter. Only Orange, Maroon, Orchid, Pink, and Yellow survived. Now there were nine puppies and three big dogs with free run of the yard. In the house, all of the puppies were confined to a small area using a couple of exercise pens that were put together. The big dogs could go anywhere in the house, but Hope chose to spend most of her time in the living room on the couch.

Hope Returns

Hope had some health issues that needed to be taken care of as soon as the puppies could leave her. After her puppies were weaned, Hope went to another foster home. At the new foster home Hope would be able to get some medication without any possibility of her puppies getting it through her milk.

Hope's puppies stayed with us until they were adopted. Mom and Dad said that these five puppies, as well as the original four, were a sad looking bunch when they first came to live with them. Now, just a couple of months later, Mom will tell anyone that all of the puppies are so beautiful. Dad thinks so too, but he will not admit it.

It was in October that the first of my little playmates was adopted. Then one after another they went to their new homes until only Orange and I were left to play with our big brothers, Comet and Bro.

It's time for some more pictures. Follow me.

The Puppy Who Refused To Die

September 25, 2005
Puppy pile on the stuffed toys

September 28, 2005
Give me that rope bone

October 04, 2005
I can sleep on Amber's shoulder

October 04, 2005
Andrea's got me, what can I do

The Puppy Who Refused To Die

October 04, 2005
Free to sleep in the Dining Room

October 11, 2005
It's pretty comfortable on this back porch

October 11, 2005
I love my stuffed animals

October 13, 2005
Relaxing with the stuffed toys

The Puppy Who Refused To Die

October 13, 2005
This belly makes a nice soft head rest

October 14, 2005
Look out, Sponge Bob is attacking

October 17, 2005
One stick for three puppies

October 24, 2005
Togetherness is good

7

Snap, Crackle, And Pop

Snap, crackle, and pop are good sounds for a breakfast cereal, but when these sounds started coming from my chest there was more than a little cause for concern. It was August 13, 2005 when the veterinarian diagnosed me with Pneumonia and Dyspnea. You can read about both Pneumonia and Dyspnea in Appendix III at the back of this book.

I had been to the doctor just two weeks earlier at which time I was treated again for coccidiosis. This Pneumonia was a new thing, it caused me to have trouble breathing, and the noises were not good.

The doctor prescribed some medicine immediately and ordered a return visit in two weeks. There would be many more visits to the veterinary clinic and many medications and treatments in attempting to make me better.

It was near the end of October when Dr. Anna said I would need inhalation treatment. A machine would be needed to allow me to inhale drugs directly into my lungs. We needed to find a machine

and these treatments could be ordered.
My old friend Joyce began a search.
Joyce looked everywhere in the valley
for the machine that I needed with no
luck. The local pharmacies would not
sell a nebulizer for use on a dog and
the pet shops just did not sell them.
Joyce turned to Ebay where a seller was
happy to provide a nebulizer for my use.

The next obstacle was adapting the
machine for use on my little snout. Dad
said he would take care of that and set
about the task. It was important that I
inhale as much of the medication as
possible to help my lungs. Something
needed to direct the medication to my
nose or mouth.

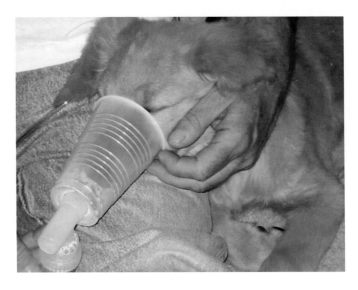

Dad made a contraption using a
plastic glass that would seal over my

face and direct all the medication through my nose and directly to my lungs. Dr. Anna found the medication she wanted me to have at a local equine veterinary center where Mom and Dad were to pick it up. The proper dosage was added to sterile saline and the machine made it safe for me to breathe.

I required two treatments a day, each lasting twenty to fifty minutes depending mostly on how well I would cooperate. Mom and Dad made many visits to the equine veterinary center in Gilbert, AZ., being asked on almost every visit "What kind of a horse do you have".

Along with the inhaled medicine I received numerous other medications, many came from Dr Anna's office, others from local pharmacies, and still more from mail order pharmacies.

With all the medicines and treatments I was receiving my condition was not improving. Even the nebulizer was not making a difference.

8

I See A Specialist

2005 was coming to an end. The holidays were just ahead when I went to see the specialist. This doctor was an expert in internal medicine. She worked out of an office in Gilbert, AZ. Again the drive to this office did not take long from my home in Mesa.

Dr. Anna had referred me to this specialist for further evaluation of my lungs. She also wanted an opportunity to brainstorm with the specialist about a cure for my lung issues. With the help of the specialist I hoped that I would get better.

My appointment was for early in the morning and I would be there for the entire day. Tests would be run that would require me to be knocked out with something called anesthesia. Mom and Dad dropped me off early and planned on returning for me before the office closed for the day.

It was not more than a couple of hours later when Mom received the call from the specialist's office. There were complications that did not allow the testing to be done. The doctor wanted her and Dad to leave plenty of time to talk when they came to pick me up. I was ready to go home at any time.

I was led into a little room where Mom, Dad, and the doctor had already gathered. It was in this room that the specialist would talk to Mom, Dad, and Me about my health.

It was not good news that I heard that day. The pneumonia was actually a secondary issue. X-rays taken at the office this morning revealed the underlying cause of my poor health. I was diagnosed with pulmonary bullae (bubbles in my lungs that could burst at any time). Because of the condition of my lungs I can not be put under anesthesia or I might die.

I was told that I would probably not make it through the holidays, and if I did, certainly I would not live past my first birthday. Mom and Dad were given a list containing phone numbers and addresses of emergency veterinary hospitals in the area. They were told that because of my condition they should not try any extreme measures; but rather to have the doctor help me go peacefully.

Mom and Dad were very sad; they had tears in their eyes. I did my best to console them that day. I can only hope it was enough.

I See A Specialist

I almost forgot! It's time for some more pictures!

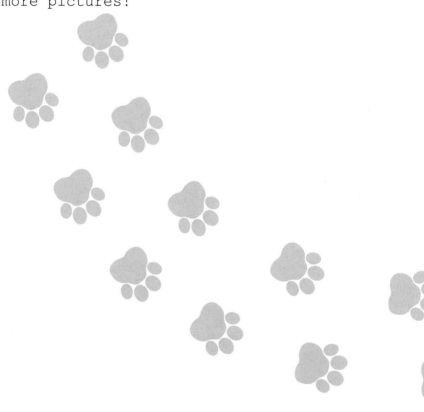

The Puppy Who Refused To Die

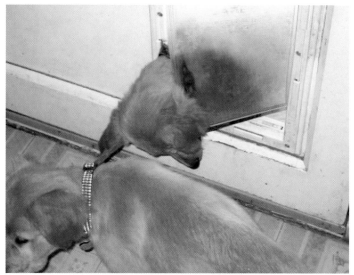

November 06, 2005
Look out - In coming

November 11, 2005
Is there room for one more

November 14, 2005
The fresh air just knocks us out

November 16, 2005
Let's line up in the bedroom

9

Where Have All the Puppies Gone

My litter mates have all been adopted. They have all changed their names. I have not talked with any of them since they moved on, except for Gus (Red), maybe once or twice, when he came home for a visit.

I will always remember all of them as they were in October of 2005, just before they moved away.

Grey (Sometimes called Princess Puppy or Prinny) is now called Honey. Her new mom and dad are Wendy and Reid.

Red knew Kas was his from the start. She had been there to help with so many things; and as the Adoption Team Coordinator, she found new homes for all the puppies and their mommas. Red became Gus when he went to live with Kas.

When Sammy lived with us I knew him as Cream. He was adopted by Erin and Chris.

Yellow decided her name should be Maggie when she moved in with Janet and Mike.

Maroon wanted to be known as Charm; Cindy and Gary were very happy to have Charm stay with them.

Orchid went with a Christmas name (Holly). She is living with her new Mom and Dad Jennifer and Michael.

Ellen and Robert adopted Pink. She changed her name to Zoe a short time later.

In December of 2005 Sue and Paul adopted Orange and Me. We both knew that they would. We now call Orange Bumpkin or Bump for short. Mom still thinks his name should be Pumpkin, but, what kind of a name is Pumpkin for a dog; we would be calling him Pump for short.

I still use the name Green, although Mom and Dad call me Mr. Green most of the time. Mom sometimes likes to call me Mr. Green Jeans. I don't know why, I have never worn pants of any kind.

Here are some pictures of my sisters and brothers shortly before we were adopted. They were taken by Mom and Dad.

The Puppy Who Refused To Die

Grey
Now called Honey

Red
Became known as Gus

Sammy
I knew him as Cream

Yellow
Decided her name should be Maggie

Maroon
Wanted to be known as Charm

Orchid
Went with a Christmas Name (Holly)

Where Have All The Puppies Gone

Pink
Changed her name to Zoe

Orange
We now call Orange Bumpkin or Bump for short

10

Not Quite My Birthday

It started in the evening, on June 18, 2006; less than two months before my first birthday. I just did not have the energy I should. My temperature was at 102 degrees, within the normal range of 100.5 to 102.5, and I was eating and drinking, so there was not too much cause for concern.

As usual, Mom woke up early the next morning. Because of the way I had been acting the night before, she checked my temperature right away. It was 104 degrees; now that is way too high! She decided I would be going to the doctor's office as soon as it opened.

It was nine o'clock in the morning by the time we could see the doctor. My temperature was now at 105.2 degrees. The vet techs went right to work putting alcohol on my paws. Within an hour my temperature had come down to 104.3.

The vet techs took some of my blood and a test called a CBC was done. The CBC showed that my white blood cell count was 40,000. It had never been this high before, and it was way over the normal range of 6,000 to 17,000 per microliter of blood. This was a clear indication that I had some kind of infection again.

Other blood tests showed that I did not have Lyme disease, tick fever, or heartworm. My lungs sounded pretty good, but we needed to knock out whatever was causing this infection before it developed into pneumonia again.

I was given three medicines to take, two that I had never taken before. Dr. Anna had been waiting to give me one of these medicines for a long time, but she said it would have interfered with my development. Now I was so close to my first birthday, I could use it.

By later in the day my temperature was 103 degrees. Dr Anna had told Mom and Dad that if I stayed below 105 for the next couple of days it would be okay. If my temperature went to 105 or over, I needed to be cooled down by putting alcohol on my paws, or by putting me into a tub of cool water.

The next couple of days were very hard on Mom; she was keeping a close eye on me. I did not want to eat or drink, but I did with a little encouragement. My temperature remained on the high side, and I had very little energy.

Then on June 21, my temperature was down to 101.5 degrees. I started to eat and drink on my own again. My energy level was higher, and I think I was

feeling a little bit better. I know Mom
was feeling a whole lot better. Because
I had been spending a lot of time next
to her in the office; I could tell.

By nine-thirty in the evening my
temperature had come down to 100
degrees. Mom thinks that is the lowest I
have ever been; she sure is happy. Now
Mom was able to sleep soundly through
the night and when she was not up by
five o'clock in the morning, I barked to
let her know it was time to play.

11

The New Medicine

My response to the new medicine was better than anyone had expected. Within a few days I was full of energy and my temperature was remaining low. I started to gain weight quickly and the noises in my lungs began to disappear. It was working! I finally was able to run, jump, and play without trouble breathing or running out of energy.

I learned how to play hard with Comet, Bro and Bumpkin, but it was Bump who I liked to play with the most. Although he had surpassed me in size, he was close to my age, and we enjoyed the same type of activities. We would run and jump on each other, or race around the yard; we would grab each other by the ears or neck and turn in circles. I was having the time of my life.

This medicine, however, was not a miracle drug; I was not cured. While I was taking the medicine I felt great but when I stopped taking my medicine it would not be long before I had no energy, no appetite, and no playfulness left in me.

The Puppy Who Refused To Die

I had more episodes where I would feel bad and more trips to see Dr. Anna. I felt good most of the time, but when I felt bad, I really felt bad. I would not eat or drink and my temperature would get very high.

I could not take the medicine every day of my life, but something could be done. I can do something the doctor calls pulse therapy. I can take the medicine for one week each month and go medicine free for the rest of the month.

Mom and Dad said this was worth a try so we started to do it. Mom decided the first week of the month would be the time for my therapy. For the remainder of the month I would go without any medication.

We will test this new system, but only time will tell if it works.

12

Who Am I?

It has been almost a year now since I was born. It took me a long time to find out who I am.

I am Green; one of nine very lucky puppies who had angels watching over them. Angels in the form of volunteers for a Golden Retriever rescue organization. Angels that removed us from the animal control facility and took us to live with Sue and Paul. Angels that provided needed supplies, and Angels that prayed for our survival. There were so many that watched over us, so many that I have never met, and so many that were there by my side when I needed them.

I am Green; one of nine puppies saved from the Pima County Animal Control Facility in Tucson, AZ. near the end of July in 2005.

I am Green; one of twenty-two puppies born; one of four that survived.

I am Green; the puppy with the chest that goes snap, crackle, and pop.

The Puppy Who Refused To Die

    I am Green; the puppy that a
specialist said would probably not live
through the holidays in 2005.
    I am Green; the same Green that
stood near deaths door for the first
year of my life.

But mostly

I am Green

The Puppy Who Refused To Die

Now it's time for more pictures of me!

Who Am I?

The Puppy Who Refused To Die

August 05, 2005
My eyes have not opened yet

August 11, 2005
This is a nice, soft blanket

Who Am I?

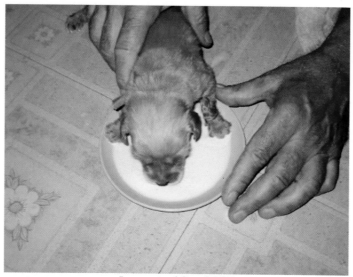

August 11, 2005
I have my own saucer of milk

August 21, 2005
What a comfortable spot

The Puppy Who Refused To Die

September 07, 2005
What are you holding me up for

September 09, 2005
I am climbing out of the tunnel

Who Am I?

September 24, 2005
What

September 28, 2005
Me and my alligator pillow

The Puppy Who Refused To Die

November 12, 2005
The bed is a good place for a puppy

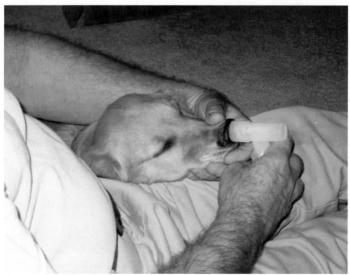

December 04, 2005
Breathe in, Breathe out

Who Am I?

December 05, 2005
I am the King of the Table

January 15, 2006
Water is good, Baths are bad

The Puppy Who Refused To Die

January 29, 2006
What are you looking at

March 11, 2006
You can call me mud dog

Who Am I?

April 24, 2006
What's a puppy got to do to get a belly rub

June 20, 2006
Bump is always getting in my face

13

Green Grows Up

For many months the pulse therapy worked. There were a couple of times when I felt sick just before it was time to start my next round of antibiotics, but there were only a couple of days left before I could be on them.

The first week of every month was the time set aside for the medicine and that was when I would have it. This system worked well until December of 2007.

Here are some pictures of me taken between July of 2006 and December of 2007.

Green Grows Up

The Puppy Who Refused To Die

July 13, 2006
What's up Mom

September 10, 2006
I can twist like a snake

December 24, 2006
I'm going to school with the kids

March 11, 2007
King of the couch

The Puppy Who Refused To Die

May 01, 2007
Relaxing on the back patio

August 06, 2007
It's my stuffed duck

December 13, 2007
I'll just stay in the Bathroom

December 18, 2007
I really don't feel good

14

Is This The End?

Tuesday December 11, 2007 was a beautiful day. Mom had the day off and Dad did not go into work until after one p.m. Mom and Dad woke up and got ready to go out. They always had some things they had to take care of but it did not take too long.

Both Bumpkin and I got our harnesses on after which we had our leashes attached. Comet and Bro do not wear harnesses and had their leashes attached directly to their collars. Mom and Dad grabbed some bags, put on their hats and coats, and off we went for our walk.

I took my normal position in the lead. I know the way. We did not take a long walk that day, the weather had been rainy and the canal walk would have been muddy. We were home before long. Mom fed and watered all the animals while Dad made breakfast for Mom and himself.

After breakfast Mom and Dad sat down on their couches, Mom on her side of the room and Dad on his. I jumped up on Dad's lap. I had something to tell him. "I am shaking and I can not stop". We just sat there for a few minutes, Dad and I, neither of us knew just what to think of this.

Mom got out the thermometer and checked my temperature. It was 101.5 degrees. She called the veterinarians office and told them what was happening. They suggested I be monitored and come in at my quarterly checkup which was in two days. If my temperature went over 102.5 or my condition changed for the worse Mom and Dad were to bring me in earlier or go to an emergency room.

I spent time with Mom that afternoon. The shaking continued on and off but my temperature was not too high. At ten p.m. Comet, Bro, Bumpkin and I all jumped into the back of the car to go pick up Dad at work.

Wednesday morning, December 12, Mom woke up and took my temperature. It was 103.5 and it was hours before Dr. Anna's office would open. She put rubbing alcohol on my paws to cool me down. With my temperature down to 102.5 about an hour later Mom put more alcohol on my paws. By eight a.m. my temperature had lowered to 101.3 degrees.

Mom called the doctor's office as soon as they opened and was able to get an appointment for three-thirty that afternoon. During the day my condition worsened. I started to stumble as I walked, I had trouble getting up, I wobbled as I stood still, and I did not want to turn my head.

At the doctor's office I met Dr. Scott, the owner of the veterinary clinic. He examined me, did some test with my legs, tested my response by pinching my skin, and stated that I have a neurological condition. My brain is not telling my legs what to do. Dr. Scott suspected a space occupying mass in the left side of my brain. My prognosis is not good.

Blood is again drawn in an attempt to determine if this condition is caused by tick fever, lyme disease, or valley fever. Mom and Dad are given medication for valley fever, the other choices have been ruled out by the results of the blood test. The blood will have to go to another lab to determine if Valley Fever is indeed the cause.

After returning home I was given my first dose of medication. It is to be administered twice a day. I have no interest in eating any of the kibble, but I gobble up a can of beef and vegetable soup when Dad places it in front of me.

It is a restless night for everyone in the family. After tossing and turning for a while, Dad went out to sleep on the couch with me right behind. Dad helped me onto the couch and I stayed with him for a long time. Sometime later, I decided to sleep on a blanket on the floor and Dad went back to bed.

Is This The End?

It was not long before I showed up at Dad's side of the bed and woke him up. I was cold to the touch and he could tell that I had been outside. Dad helped me onto the bed and covered me with a blanket. I shook again and I could not stop.

On Thursday morning December 13, while Mom and Dad took their showers I stayed in the bathroom on a towel. This was my normal spot when Mom would shower but I usually did not stay while Dad was in there.

Mom and Dad got dressed, went into the dining room and put on Bumpkin's harness and leash. Then they put on Comet and Bro's leashes, and wiped the tears from their eyes when I came into the room and sat down in position to get my harness. Dad put on my harness and leash. I walked out the door with my family, and walked ever so slowly for about a block before they turned around and brought me back home.

On Friday December 14, Mom and Dad both had to go to work. Dad left early to be to work by seven a.m. and Mom stayed for just a short time before leaving for work herself. I was on my own but not alone. Comet, Bro, and Bumpkin were there to keep me company. Still the day is long and boring, I cannot run, I can not jump, I can not play, and I have little interest in the toys that lay all over the house.

The Puppy Who Refused To Die

Mom was the first one to come home today. We spent time together on the couch. Dad was home before it was dark and said we should go for a walk. I was ready and took my position in the dining room waiting for my harness.

As Dad harnessed Bumpkin and me, Mom prepared Comet and Bro. We took a route that allowed me to walk six blocks, and I even trotted a little along the way. I did not try to take the lead. Dad thinks I no longer know the way.

It was a good day. I walked with my family and later spent time on the couch with Mom and with Dad.

Saturday December 15, was uneventful. Dad started work at seven a.m. and did not get home until after four that afternoon. Mom had an event to attend for the rescue group she now is associated with. Bumpkin was able to go with; he was the star for the day.

I was feeling much better when Dad got home. I met him at the door, hopped on my hind legs, and barked for attention. These are all things I could not do just a few days ago.

Dad found a message on the machine from Dr. Scott. I do not have valley fever, the medicine can be stopped. Dr Scott had received a progress report that Mom had left for him. He commented on how happy he was that I was doing

Is This The End?

better and he wants Mom and Dad to give him another progress report on Monday.

It was three a.m. on Sunday December 16, when I jumped on the bed and woke Dad up. Once again I was shaking and I could not stop. Dad covered me with a blanket and put his arm around me. A short time later I quit shaking and slept soundly with Dad until he woke up at five-thirty.

Not long after we got up Mom, Dad, Comet, Bro, Bumpkin and I were all in the kitchen when suddenly something was attacking me. I was quickly turning in circles, barking, and growling. The other dogs came close but Mom and Dad led them to the back door and locked them in the yard. I was going to tear apart whatever it was that was attacking me even if no one else could see it.

Dad had followed the doctor's instructions; I had not received my medicine last night. In the off chance that the medication was doing me some good even though I do not have valley fever, Dad gave me my morning dose as soon as I had calmed down.

It only took a few minutes before Mom was able to calm me down but then I wanted to be alone. I hid under the table in Bumpkins protected spot. It is safe there. Tomorrow Mom and Dad will call for another appointment with Dr. Scott.

Monday was rather quiet although I did walk with my family for about one mile. I no longer have any interest in taking the lead. I hung out in the back of the pack walking with my Dad.

Tuesday December 18, the doctor was able to see me early in the morning. More blood was drawn as well as some urine for further testing. I quit taking all medications so we can see what affect it will have upon me. Mom and Dad will be keeping a close eye on me.

Tuesday evening Dad has time before he goes into work for a meeting. Bumpkin and I are harnessed up and all of us are put on leashes. Once again I get to walk with my family. Mom takes Bumpkin and Bro and goes out first. Dad has Comet and me. As soon as I am out of the house I race to take the lead. Although Comet keeps sticking his big head in front of me, I could take the lead; once again I know the way.

Only time will tell if I will completely recover. I may get better or I may get worse, but no matter what happens, I know that Mom and Dad will be there. I will not be alone.

Is This The End?

Animal Rescue

I believe in animal rescue and encourage you to get involved.

Animal rescue groups were created to assist almost any type of animal that you could imagine. To find out more about organizations in your area check on the internet, or ask questions at your local animal control facility.

Here is a list of a few of the organizations that are located in Arizona. I am sure there are many, many more; you just need to take a little time to find them.

I do not endorse any of these organizations. I simply located them by looking on the internet.

LOCATION	TYPE	BREED	URL
Maricopa County	All	All	http://www.animalrescuecenter.net/
Arizona	All	All	http://www.aawl.org/
Arizona	All	All	http://www.azfriends.org/
Pima County	All	All	http://www.faircares.org/
Arizona	All	All	http://www.morningstarr.org/
Arizona	Birds	All	http://www.the-oasis.org/

Arizona	Cats/Dogs	All	http://www.azrescue.org/
Sun City	Cats/Dogs	All	http://www.sunvalleypets.org/
Maricopa County	Cats/Dogs	All	http://www.pawplacement.org/
Arizona	Dogs	Small Dogs	http://www.notsograndedogs.org/
Arizona	Dogs	Australian Cattle Dogs	http://www.newhopecattledogs.com/
Arizona	Dogs	Australian Shepherd	http://www.petfinder.com/shelters/CA562.html
Arizona	Dogs	Basset Hound	http://www.azbassetrescue.com/
Arizona	Dogs	Beagle	http://www.azbeaglerescue.com/metadot/index.pl
Arizona	Dogs	Border Collie	Theresa, jfhwts@i-love-dogs.com
Arizona	Dogs	Boxer	http://www.arizonaboxerrescue.org/water/default.asp?x=1&DID=1320
Arizona	Dogs	Cairn Terrier	http://www.southwestcairnrescue.com/
Arizona	Dogs	Chesapeake Bay Retrievers	http://www.azrr.org/
Arizona	Dogs	Chinese Crested	http://www.rmccr.org/index.htm
Arizona	Dogs	Curly Coated Retrievers	http://www.azrr.org/
Arizona	Dogs	Dachshund	http://www.notsograndedogs.org/
Arizona	Dogs	Dachshund	http://www.3drescue.org/index.php
Arizona	Dogs	Doberman	http://www.3drescue.org/index.php
Arizona	Dogs	Flat Coated Retrievers	http://www.azrr.org/
Arizona	Dogs	Golden Retrievers	http://www.azrr.org/

Arizona	Dogs	Golden Retrievers	http://cc.usu.edu/~nancyr/golden/cgrr.html
Arizona	Dogs	Great Dane	http://www.3drescue.org/index.php
Arizona	Dogs	Great Dane	http://www.petfinder.com/shelters/azdanerescue.html
Arizona	Dogs	Great Dane	http://www.azdanesaversrescueadoptions.com/
Arizona	Dogs	Greyhound	http://www.gpa-az.com/
Arizona	Dogs	Italian Greyhound	http://www.midwestigrescue.com/contacts.html
Arizona	Dogs	Labrador Retriever	http://www.dlrrphoenix.org/
Arizona	Dogs	Nova Scotia Duck Tolling Retrievers	http://www.azrr.org/
Arizona	Dogs	Retrievers	http://www.azrr.org/
Phoenix Area	Dogs	Rottweiler	http://www.phxrottrescue.org/
Central Arizona	Dogs	Samoyed	http://www.geocities.com/azsammyrescue/
Arizona	Dogs	Sheltie	Theresa, jfhwts@i-love-dogs.com
Arizona	Dogs	Siberian Husky	http://www.ashra.org/
Arizona	Dogs	Staffordshire Bull Terrier	http://www.geocities.com/oasisrescue/
Arizona	Ferrets	All	http://members.tripod.com/FerretFriends/
Arizona	Ferrets	All	http://www.ferretfriends.org/
Arizona	Ferrets	All	http://www.geocities.com/ferretcorneraz
Arizona	Ferrets	All	http://www.morningstarr.org/
Arizona	Potbellied Pigs	All	http://www.ironwoodpigsanctuary.org/
Arizona	Rabbits	Domestic	http://www.bhrabbitrescue.org/

Appendix I Charts

These charts are the records of Sue and Paul. Care was taken to insure the information in these charts was accurately reproduced using the original handwritten notes.

Note: one tablespoon = fifteen ML

At Intake July 31

Dark Purple	Red	Cream	Lavender	White	Blue	Green	Grey	Brown
Male	Male	Male	Female	Female	Female	Male	Female	Male
13 oz	12.5 oz	13 oz	10.5 oz	10.5 oz	10 oz	14.5 oz	13 oz	13 oz

July 31 p.m. hours

	5	8
White	08 ml	08 ml
Green	16 ml	04 ml
Grey	16 ml	04 ml
Brown	08 ml	08 ml

August 01 a.m. hours

	12:00	04:30	08:30	Weight	11:00
White	08 ml	08 ml	08 ml	10 oz	04 ml
Green	12 ml	12 ml	08 ml	14.5 oz	08 ml
Grey	12 ml	12 ml	32 ml	13 oz	
Brown	08 ml	08 ml	16 ml	12.5 oz	

August 01 p.m. hours

	12:15	02:15	05:00	07:15	09:15	10:15
White		08 ml		7.5 ml	05 ml	
Green	02 ml	15 ml	15 ml	3.5 ml		05 ml
Grey	16 ml	22 ml		25 ml		10 ml
Brown	02 ml	15 ml		23 ml		7.5 ml

August 02 a.m. hours

	12:15	04:30	06:30	07:45	Weight	09:00	11:00
White	15 ml	7.5 ml	7.5 ml		10 oz	04 ml	7.5 ml
Green		14 ml		10 ml	14 oz		10 ml
Grey		25 ml		15 ml	12.5 oz		28 ml
Brown		15 ml		20 ml	14 oz		07 ml

August 02 p.m. hours

	01:30	02:30	03:30	05:30	07:30	08:30	09:45
White	06 ml		05 ml	10 ml	7.5 ml		12 ml
Green		10 ml		20 ml		7.5 ml	
Grey		13 ml		15 ml		15 ml	
Brown		15 ml		20 ml		15 ml	

August 03 a.m. hours

	12:30	04:00	Weight	06:00	07:00	08:00	10:15	11:00
White	07 ml	10 ml	10 oz	7.5 ml		8.5 ml		06 ml
Green	15 ml	10 ml	14 oz		10 ml		15 ml	
Grey	20 ml	30 ml	12.5 oz		12 ml		23 ml	
Brown	30 ml	12 ml	13 oz		22 ml		08 ml	

August 03 p.m. hours

	01:00	03:00	04:15	Weight	07:15	09:45
White	12 ml	14 ml		10.5 oz	05 ml	13 ml
Green	16 ml		10 ml	14 oz	7.5 ml	20 ml
Grey	14 ml		17 ml	12 oz	30 ml	10 ml
Brown	22 ml		05 ml	13 oz	7.5 ml	7.5 ml

The first visit with Dr Anna was on August 01, at five p.m. for puppies White, Green, Grey and Brown.

August 04 a.m. hours

	01:30	04:30	06:45	Weight	09:15	11:15
White	08 ml	09 ml	12 ml	10 oz	08 ml	10 ml
Green	20 ml	30 ml		15 oz	14 ml	
Grey	30 ml	12 ml		12 oz	30 ml	
Brown	15 ml	10 ml		13 oz	10 ml	

August 04 p.m. hours

	12:30	01:15	03:15	Weight	06:00	09:00
White		10 ml	13 ml	9.5 oz	13 ml	12 ml
Green	10 ml		22 ml	14.5 oz	15 ml	05 ml
Grey	20 ml		25 ml	12.5 oz	32 ml	02 ml
Brown	05 ml		25 ml	13 oz	07 ml	07 ml
Red				14.5 oz	10 ml	10 ml
Cream				14 oz	05 ml	7.5 ml

August 05 a.m. hours

	01:30	05:00	07:45	Weight	08:45
White	15 ml	14 ml	10 ml	Died	
Green	08 ml	22 ml		14.5 oz	28 ml
Grey	25 ml	20 ml		12.5 oz	30 ml
Brown	15 ml	13 ml		12.5 oz	09 ml
Red	20 ml	15 ml		15 oz	15 ml
Cream	20 ml	11 ml		15 oz	08 ml

August 05 p.m. hours

	12:30	Temp	04:00	07:00	10:00
Green	21 ml	99.9	42 ml	01 ml	18 ml
Grey	05 ml	99.9	30 ml	05 ml	13 ml
Brown	08 ml	100	15 ml	15 ml	15 ml
Red	10 ml	98.8	15 ml	28 ml	
Cream	08 ml	98.8	10 ml	15 ml	7.5 ml

Red and Cream returned to Sue and Paul's care on August 04, in the early afternoon. Both had shown improvement with Red increasing in weight by two full ounces and Cream gaining one ounce.

August 06 a.m. hours

	01:30	05:15	Temp	Weight	08:45	11:45
Green	22 ml	25 ml	100.4	1#	28 ml	22 ml
Grey	17 ml	7.5 ml	101.2	12 oz	40 ml	
Brown	12 ml	Died				
Red	21 ml	28 ml	100.7	1#	16 ml	15 ml
Cream	22 ml	14 ml	99.4	15 oz	16 ml	15 ml

August 06 p.m. hours

	02:45	05:30	07:30	Weight	08:30
Green		22 ml		1#	28 ml
Grey	15 ml	30 ml		12 oz	09 ml
Red	15 ml	15 ml	17 ml	1#	
Cream	15 ml	22 ml		15 oz	30 ml

August 07 a.m. hours

	12:30	04:00	Weight	Temp	Meds	7:45	10:45
Green	15 ml	32 ml	1# 1 oz	98.2		29 ml	8 ml
Grey	32 ml	10 ml	13 oz	99.8		22 ml	
Red	24 ml	35 ml	1#	99.5	X	30 ml	30 ml
Cream		24 ml	1#	99.8	X	20 ml	14 ml

August 07 p.m. hours

	01:45	04:45	Weight	07:45
Green	20 ml	30 ml	1# 1.5 oz	15 ml
Grey	25 ml	16 ml	13.5 oz	15 ml
Red	20 ml	45 ml	1# 2 oz	05 ml
Cream	16 ml	7.5 ml	1#	15 ml

Records were not kept on the dispensing of medication to the entire litter of puppies. The entire litter was treated multiple times for parasites, coccidiosis giardia, and worms, often with doctor ordered OTC medication. When medication was ordered for less than the entire litter a column labeled Meds will indicate that the medicine was dispensed to that puppy or puppies.

August 08 a.m. hours

	12:00	04:30	Weight	Temp	09:00
Green	20 ml	13 ml	1# 1 oz	100.7	15 ml
Grey	28 ml	17 ml	13 oz	101.3	30 ml
Red	28 ml	37 ml	1# 1.5 oz	100.8	30 ml
Cream	30 ml	22 ml	1# 1 oz	100.3	16 ml

August 08 p.m. hours

	12:00	03:00	04:30	06:30	Weight	09:30
Green	29 ml			18 ml	1# 2 oz	07 ml
Grey	06 ml	17.5 ml		7.5 ml	14.5 oz	37 ml
Red	29 ml	16 ml		16 ml	1# 2 oz	24 ml
Cream	16 ml		15 ml	03 ml	1# 1 oz	16 ml

August 09 a.m. hours

	01:30	05:30	Weight	Temp	08:20	11:30
Green	30 ml	23 ml	1# 3 oz	99.1	16 ml	25 ml
Grey	17 ml	30 ml	15.5 oz	99.1	02 ml	32 ml
Red	35 ml	32 ml	1# 3 oz	98.8	10 ml	30 ml
Cream	20 ml	25 ml	1# 1.5 oz	99.1		30 ml

August 09 p.m. hours

	02:30	04:45	07:00	09:15
Green	42 ml	27.5 ml		30 ml
Grey	24 ml		18 ml	01 ml
Red	47 ml		14 ml	30 ml
Cream	20 ml	32.5 ml		17 ml

August 10 a.m. hours

	12:45	04:30	Weight	07:30	10:30
Green	30 ml	17 ml	1.25 #	32 ml	30 ml
Grey	44 ml	12 ml	15.5 oz	29 ml	10 ml
Red	43 ml	19 ml	1.25 #	40 ml	15 ml
Cream	37 ml	13 ml	1.025 #	21 ml	12 ml

August 10 p.m. hours

	01:30	04:30	06:00	08:45
Green	35 ml	35 ml		30 ml
Grey	58 ml		14 ml	25 ml
Red	45 ml	20 ml		30 ml
Cream	33 ml		31 ml	22 ml

August 11 a.m. hours

	01:00	05:00	07:00	09:00
Green	15 ml	14 ml	1# 6 oz	31 ml
Grey	30 ml	14 ml	1# 1 oz	28 ml
Red	36 ml	25 ml	1# 6 oz	25 ml
Cream	31 ml	18 ml	1# 4 oz	45 ml

August 11 p.m. hours

	12:00	04:00	08:00
Green	35 ml	30 ml	30 ml
Grey	29 ml	25 ml	15 ml
Red	35 ml	45 ml	39 ml
Cream	22.5 ml	45 ml	20 ml

August 12

	12:00	04:20	Weight	Meds	18:15	12:15	04:00	08:00
Green	40 ml	60 ml	1# 9 oz	X		38 ml	15 ml	58 ml
Grey	44.5 ml	40 ml	1# 4 oz		30 ml		15 ml	54 ml
Red	55 ml	60 ml	1# 9 oz	X	08 ml	40 ml	50 ml	50 ml
Cream	40 ml	40 ml	1# 6 oz	X	29 ml	28 ml	60 ml	15 ml

August 13

	12:00	04:30	Meds	Weight	08:30	12:30	04:30	08:30
Green	15 ml	60 ml	X	1# 11 oz	35 ml	45 ml	12 ml	35 ml
Grey	15 ml	60 ml		1# 6 oz	17 ml	30 ml	16 ml	35 ml
Red	30 ml	60 ml	X	1# 11 oz	35 ml	60 ml	16 ml	61 ml
Cream	47 ml	45 ml	X	1# 9 oz	25 ml	43 ml	33 ml	30 ml

August 14

	12:30	04:30	Weight	Meds	08:30	12:30	05:00	09:00
Green	30 ml	49 ml	1# 12 oz	X	03 ml	70 ml		75 ml
Grey	22 ml	30 ml	1# 7 oz		30 ml	75 ml	7.5 ml	50 ml
Red	60 ml	61 ml	1# 14 oz	X	60 ml	70 ml	45 ml	55 ml
Cream	60 ml	45 ml	1# 10 oz	X	46 ml	70 ml	28 ml	45 ml

August 15

	01:30	05:30	Weight	Meds	09:30	01:30	05:30	09:30
Green		75 ml	2#	X		25 ml	25 ml	75 ml
Grey	32 ml	25 ml	1# 9 oz		45 ml	20 ml	27 ml	75 ml
Red	75 ml	50 ml	2# 2 oz	X	40 ml	50 ml	60 ml	30 ml
Cream	25 ml	72 ml	1# 15 oz			75 ml	62 ml	45 ml

Green and Red received shots while at the veterinarian's office on August 15, for moisture in their lungs.

August 16

	04:15	Weight	08:30	12:30	04:30	Meds	08:30
Green	65 ml	2# 1 oz	20 ml	50 ml	100 ml	X	
Grey	50 ml	1# 11 oz	25 ml	60 ml	20 ml		60 ml
Red	85 ml	2# 2 oz	25 ml	100 ml	78 ml	X	75 ml
Cream	100 ml	2#	30 ml	100 ml	05 ml	X	50 ml

August 17

	04:30	Weight	Meds	08:30	12:30	05:30	09:30
Green	80 ml	2# 3 oz	X	100 ml	30 ml	26 ml	110 ml
Grey	70 ml	1# 15.5 oz		60 ml	25 ml	60 ml	30 ml
Red	110 ml	2# 8 oz	X	45 ml	90 ml	50 ml	100 ml
Cream	110 ml	2# 5 oz	X	50 ml		115 ml	

August 18

	05:00	Weight	09:00	01:20	05:00	09:30
Green	85 ml	2# 6 oz	65 ml		100 ml	
Grey	55 ml	1# 15 oz	65 ml		75 ml	90 ml
Red	100 ml	2# 10 oz	60 ml	75 ml	100 ml	100 ml
Cream	125 ml	2# 7 oz	85 ml	50 ml	101 ml	75 ml

August 19

	03:30	Weight	08:00	12:00	06:00	Meds	10:00
Green	100 ml	2# 9 oz	60 ml	10 ml	85 ml	X	25 ml
Grey	50 ml	2# 1 oz	50 ml	50 ml			50 ml
Red	75 ml	2# 14 oz	100 ml	100 ml	105 ml	X	80 ml
Cream	100 ml	2# 10 oz	50 ml	125 ml	110 ml	X	35 ml

August 20

	05:00	Weight	09:00	01:00	05:00	10:00
Green	70 ml	2# 11 oz	75 ml	10 ml	75 ml	140 ml
Grey	50 ml	2# 3 oz	120 ml		25 ml	90 ml
Red	65 ml	3# 1oz	150 ml	75 ml	125 ml	125 ml
Cream	100 ml	2# 13 oz	50 ml		30 ml	120 ml

August 21

	05:15	09:30	02:00	06:00	10:00
Green	80 ml		88 ml	95 ml	70 ml
Grey	105 ml	30 ml	95 ml	50 ml	30 ml
Red	75 ml	70 ml	95 ml	130 ml	100 ml
Cream	105 ml		120 ml	50 ml	90 ml

August 22

	05:15	09:30	01:30	09:30
Green	120 ml		115 ml	02 ml
Grey		73 ml	140 ml	02 ml
Red	150 ml	80 ml	125 ml	75 ml
Cream	95 ml	85 ml	110 ml	120 ml

At one p.m. on August 18, the puppies shared a bowl of food. On August 22, at nine a.m. the puppies shared a can of food. On August 23, the puppies shared canned food mixed with kibble for two meals, one at seven-thirty a.m. and one between eight-thirty and nine-thirty p.m. At both meals a bowl of formula was provided.

They learned quickly how to make a mess, how to eat from the bowl took a little longer. After a good cleaning they were ready for their meals from a bottle.

August 23

	06:00	07:30	Weight	Meds	09:30
Green	75 ml	75 ml	3# 1 oz	X	70 ml
Grey	90 ml	75 ml	2# 12 oz	X	120 ml
Red	88 ml	60 ml	3# 11 oz	X	110 ml
Cream	85 ml	85 ml	3# 6 oz	X	120 ml

August 24

	06:00	09:30
Green	32 ml	150 ml
Grey	105 ml	100 ml
Red	85 ml	200 ml
Cream	98 ml	175 ml

The next chart gives information from a veterinarian visit of August 25. Grey was given a shot for moisture in her lungs, Green and Cream received medication for other conditions.

August 25

	Weight	Temp	Meds
Green	3# 6 oz	100.9	X
Grey	2# 15 oz	101.1	X
Red	3# 15 oz	101.4	
Cream	3# 11 oz	101.3	X

The charts changed at this point to indicate only weights. Charting continued through September 30, 2005.
The weights on September 09 were taken at the veterinarian clinic on one of the regular visits.

August 27, through August 31

	08/27	08/29	08/31
Green	3# 13 oz	4# 1 oz	4# 10 oz
Grey	4# 1 oz	4# 4 oz	4# 7 oz
Red	4# 4 oz	4# 8 oz	4# 12 oz
Cream	3# 8oz	3# 11 oz	4# 1 oz

September 01, through September 30

	09/07	09/08	09/11	09/15	09/21	09/29
Green	6#	6.3#	6.5#	7.5#	9.5#	11.9#
Grey	6#	6.3#	7.0#	7.75#	9#	10.6#
Red	6.5#	6.9#	8.0#	8.5#	10#	12.7#
Cream	6#	5.9 #	6.5#	7#	8.5#	11.2#

Hope had come back to stay with Sue and Paul. Here is a chart showing the weights for her puppies in late September.

September Weights for Hope's litter

	09/21	09/30
Yellow	6.25#	7.6#
Maroon	6.25#	7.8#
Orchid	5.25#	6.5#
Orange	4.5#	6#
Pink	5#	5.9#

Appendix II E-mails

From: Sue
Sent: Monday, August 01, 2005
Subject: RE: Info on puppies

Vet appointment with Dr. Anna in Chandler at 4 PM today for my four. My group smells much better. Paul gave them a good washing last night and this morning. No red anal spots that I remember but we will recheck when we check for ticks.

Grey ate 2 TBS at 8:30. White and Green are our tiny eaters. Both ate only one half TBS but their tummies were full. They ate well and eagerly but did not want more after they quit.

Brown was right at one TBS. We're going to try to get White and Green to eat more soon.

From: Sue
Sent: Monday, August 01, 2005

The Puppy Who Refused To Die

Subject: RE: Info on puppies

White is a struggle. Two lost a little weight but they were jumping around so much I might have read the scale wrong. Not a lot of weight and we are pushing the food more today. White is the one I am worried the most about. We will know more after their vet appointment at 4. Did you get an appointment with Dr. F?

From: Sue
Sent: Wednesday, August 03, 2005
Subject: Puppy update

I have an update from Mary. I am sad to say, Purple didn't make it. He passed away this morning at the doctor's office. The other four puppies are at home with Mary. They are now on Clavamox & are being wormed with Panacur. Mary has added egg yolk, mayonnaise, & yogurt to the goat's milk & is happy to report that they sucked it right down! Even Cream, her worst eater, sucked down thirty ml! The puppies hadn't eaten since seven a.m., so they were hungry, but maybe they have reached a turning point. The extra protein & fat should help with the weight gain (which has not been seen yet, unfortunately).

From: Sue
Sent: Thursday, August 04, 2005
Subject: update

I have received another update from Mary. I am sorry to report that Lavender did not make it through the night. She went to be with her brother over the Bridge sometime between ten-thirty & midnight last night.

Cream is doing the best of all right now; however that changes minute to minute. He has gained one ounce since Mary has had him. He isn't as active as the other two, but for now is holding his own.

Red has gained about one and one-half ounces, but a lot of pus was removed from his umbilicus this morning. Maybe it's finally starting to clear. Who knows, He was Mary's best eater, but has slacked off a bit.

Blue is the next biggest concern regarding survival. She has lost one ounce since she has been with Mary. She is down to 8.9 ounces. She is on two hourly feeds, but still is loosing. If Mary tries to push her too much, she vomits, so Mary is playing it by ear.

The Puppy Who Refused To Die

All of their stools are still slimy despite the Clavamox & the Panacur. If the diarrhea were to stop, they would probably gain better.

Keep these little ones in your prayers.

From: Sue
Sent: Saturday, August 20, 2005

Some folks have called Paul and I saints and angels. I'm sure others are just calling us NUTS. The new pups arrived at our house 10 PM Thursday 8/18 It took us until this morning to get things into a routine and for me to catch up on some sleep. Please keep Mint most of all in your thoughts and prayers. She is the one I am most worried about at the moment. Both girls are trying to be excellent moms but we are going to supplement Hope's litter a little bit at a time because they are very small and she is SO skinny herself.

I'm thinking the best way to keep track of these pups versus the first ones we got is to call them by the Mom's name then the color. These were their weights as of 10:30 PM 8-18 on the pups and the

official weight at the vets for the moms
on 8-19

Faith Red 35 pounds 2-1/2 years old
(estimated age)
Pups born 8-2-05 all currently dark gold
Faith - Black Male 1# 14 oz
Faith - Navy Male 1# 14 oz
Faith - Hunter Male 2# 2 oz

Hope Blonde 33.5 pounds 1-1/2 years old
(estimated age)
Pups born 8-6-05 currently all blonde
but some look like they will be light
gold

Hope - Maroon Female 1# 1oz
Hope - Yellow Female 15oz
Hope - Pink Female 13-1/2 oz
Hope - Mint Female 12oz
Hope - Orange Male 1# 1oz
Hope - Orchid Female 13 oz
Hope - Smoke Male 11oz

I understand Joyce is sending something
out on the vet visit yesterday. Basics
all are being treated for roundworm,
Hope has tick fever but can not be
treated while nursing pups, Faith has
liver issues that may clear up as we get
rid of worms and get some decent food
into her. All dogs are on antibiotics.
Faith and Hope are on daily pet multi
vitamin and will start getting ½ oz of
cooked liver 3X a week as they are very
anemic. The worm thing is contagious so

these moms and pups are in my office until they go to the long term Fosters.

My first set of pups are all doing well but my brilliant husband brought up this morning that all these pups came from the same place so we will be testing them for worms next week. I will try to send out an Ofoto album later today or tomorrow. For now know these girls are very loving and happy. They are very protective of their pups. Paul and I will do the best we possibly can for the moms and pups. Thanks for the honor of entrusting them to our care.

From: Sue
Sent: Monday, June 19, 2006
Subject: Please keep my Green Jeans in your thoughts and prayers

Mr. Green Jeans was fine most of yesterday but was acting a bit down last night. It was his normal temperature taking day and it turned out to be 102 degrees. This morning he was way quiet for him and his temp was 104 so he's going to the vet as soon as they open. I'll keep you posted. He is eating and drinking.

From: Sue
Sent: Monday, June 19, 2006
Subject: RE: Please keep my Green Jeans in your thoughts and prayers

He was up to 105.2 degrees when we got to the vet at nine a.m. Spent an hour putting alcohol on his paw pads and got it down to 104.3. He got three medications and hopefully will be feeling a lot better in a couple of days.

White count was off the charts at around 40,000. Red count is okay yet. Clear for Heartworm, Lyme and Tick fever. The Doctor thinks it is just part of his poor immune system and luckily we know what to watch for. So far the lungs are not sounding too bad so hopefully we will knock out what ever is causing the infection before he gets pneumonia again.

The good news is that he is old enough now to put him on a couple of different antibiotics so he is on two that he has never had before; so should not have a resistance to them.

His temp this afternoon was 103.9 degrees — The doctor told me it could stay in that range for a couple of days

The Puppy Who Refused To Die

but if it gets back in the 105 area to start cooling him down with the alcohol or put him in a tub of cool water.

I'll keep you posted. Please keep him in your prayers.

From: Sue
Sent: Wednesday, June 21, 2006
Subject: Wednesday update on Mr. Green Jeans

Good news. Mr. Green Jeans' temperature is down to 101.5 degrees this morning.

Yahoo!

He's looking a lot better but still is very weak. Most of yesterday his temp was up around 103.7 so I'm sure he will need a few days to get his energy back. He is eating his canned food and drinking water on his own. Yesterday I had to coax him to do both.

I've attached a couple of pictures of Bumpkin keeping Green Jeans company right next to my desk yesterday. Bump had to be touching him to sleep so he knew when Green Jeans moved or just to comfort Green Jeans - I'm not sure which.

Please keep the prayers and happy thoughts coming. For the people that are keeping Buddy in their prayers today I have to say he is being taken care of Dr. Anna who also has taken care of Mr. Green Jeans since he was nine days old.

I don't think either of our fur kids could be in better hands. All the vets at the Vet Clinic in Chandler are wonderful.

From: Sue
Sent: Thursday, June 22, 2006
Subject: Wiggle Butt Green Jeans is back

Just wanted everyone to know that Mr. Wiggle Butt Green Jeans woke me up this morning at five with a woof and let's play. His temp was in the 101.3 degree range most of yesterday and was down to 100 exactly last night at nine-thirty.

I think that's the first time his temp has ever been that low. We'll still be watching him closely but it looks like we caught the infection nice and early and got it kicked out of his system.

The Puppy Who Refused To Die

I'll call Dr. Anna this morning to let her know.

From: Sue
Sent: Dec 12, 2007

Yesterday Mr. Green was laying on Paul more than normal and was shivering a bit. Paul took his temp and it was 101.5 which is OK for a dog. I called Dr. Anna's office and they confirmed that. He seemed to be pretty much normal other than the shivers and being Velcroed to Paul. We chalked up the shivering to the cold rainy day and his being so skinny. We set up his normal 4 month check up for Thursday the 13th.

This morning Mr. Green is not his normal self and his temp is 103.5 – NOT GOOD for a dog. I sprayed his feet with alcohol to get the temp down and will be on the phone leaving a message for the vet at 7 and calling again at 8 if they haven't called me.

It's been so long since he's been sick but he has all the signs despite just finishing his Pulse Anti-biotic treatment on the 7th.

Appendix III Definitions

Coccidiosis

This is what Joyce told me in an E-mail.

Coccidiosis (käk sid′ē ō′sis)

General Information

Coccidiosis is a parasitic disease of
the intestinal tract caused by
microscopic organisms called coccidia.
The disease spreads from one animal to
another by contact with infected feces.
It is most severe in young or weak
animals and often causes bloody
diarrhea.

What are coccidia?

Coccidia are small protozoans (one-
celled organisms) that multiply in the
intestinal tracts of dogs and cats, most
commonly in kittens and puppies less
than six months of age, in adult animals
whose immune system is suppressed or in
animals who are stressed in other ways

(e.g., change in ownership, other
disease present).

Dyspnea

From Wikipedia, the free encyclopedia

Dyspnea or Dyspnoea (Pronounced disp-
nee-ah) is percieved to be difficulty of
breathing or painful breathing. It is a
common symptom of numerous medical
disorders.

Pneumonia-Non Human

From Wikipedia, the free encyclopedia

Pneumonia is an illness which can result
from a variety of causes, including
infection with bacteria, viruses, fungi,
or parasites. Pneumonia can occur in any
animal with lungs, including mammals,
birds, and reptiles.

Symptoms associated with pneumonia
include fever, fast or difficult
breathing, nasal discharge, and
decreased activity. Different animal
species have distinct lung anatomy and
physiology and are thus affected by
pneumonia differently. Differences in
anatomy, immune systems, diet, and
behavior also affects the particular
microorganisms commonly causing

Appendix III Definitions

pneumonia. Diagnostic tools include
physical examination, testing of the
sputum, and x-ray investigation.
Treatment depends on the cause of the
pneumonia; bacterial pneumonia is
treated with antibiotics.

From the Author

    This is the first book that I have ever written. Prior to this I just figured I had nothing to say, or at least nothing that anyone would be interested in reading about.

Paul with Green

    I am now fifty four years old and will turn fifty five before this book goes to print. I was born in a small town in Illinois (Woodstock). It was not so small that everyone there knew

everyone else, but at times it did seem
like it. I grew up in Woodstock, where I
met my wife (Susan). Susan and I were
married by a Justice of the Peace at the
County Court House in Woodstock.

We have two children, a daughter
Karen, and a son Fred. Both of our
children were born in Woodstock where we
lived until 1986. We moved to Arizona to
get away from the cold, and found Mesa
to be the place that we wanted to stay.

I have had many jobs both in
Illinois and Arizona and I have also
been in business for myself. I currently
work for a large home improvement store
in Mesa, Az. where I am an appliance
sales associate.

Our children are grown and on their
own. We have two granddaughters, Andrea
and Amber, whose pictures you will see
in this book. With the children grown
and the house empty, Susan and I became
more involved in animal rescue. We
fostered for a Golden Retriever rescue
group and quickly found ourselves to be
the owners of two extra large Golden
Retrievers named Comet and Bro.

Susan and I through our involvement
with the rescue organization later
became the foster family of a puppy
known as Green. Green inspired me to
write this story, and I tell it through
him, or he tells it through me.
Actually, I am not really certain who
was telling who.

The Puppy Who Refused To Die

The story of Green, the puppy who refused to die, is not unique. This type of story is repeated day after day in communities around the world. All types of animals are rescued from dogs, to cats, birds, rabbits, ferrets, and any other animal that you can imagine.

The costs and time needed for care of animals that have been saved can be extremely high. If you would like to help care for puppies like Green, or other animals in need, you can make a donation, or give of your time to an organization near you.

From The Author

To order copies of this book

Complete this order blank and send it to:

$\mathcal{F}$lorian $\mathcal{V}$alentine Publishing
3032 S. Paseo Loma Circle
Mesa, AZ 85202

Name:		
Address:		
City:	State:	
Zip:	Telephone:	
I want to order: The Puppy Who Refused To Die		

Quantity Ordered	Cover Price	Total
	$17.95	$
Shipping and Handling - First book		4.50
Shipping and Handling - $1.50 per additional book		
Arizona Residents must add 8.05% Sales Tax		
Total - Please send payment for total amount - Orders will not be fulfilled without proper payment		

Allow 6 weeks for all orders placed through the mail.

To receive your order faster; order online at:

florianvalentine.com

All online orders will be processed through paypal.

Becker College